— THE —
MIND
— OF THE —
STREET

Poetic Stories and
Thoughts About Present Day Times

G. J. O'LEARY

UK Book Publishing.com

Design, typesetting and publishing by UK Book Publishing

www.ukbookpublishing.com

ISBN: 978-1-917329-85-9

To see a world in a grain of sand
And a heaven in a wild flower,
To hold infinity in the palm of your hand
And eternity in an hour.

William Blake 1757-1827

For my family

PREFACE

Francis Cammack was born in 1922 in Liverpool. He was one of 7 brothers and 3 sisters. At the age of 14 he was a butcher's lad. During the Second World War Frank first served in The Home Guard and later with the Kings South Lancashire Regiment, being part of the D DAY landings on Sword Beech in June 1944. He was 21. His older brother, Charlie, was also there on D DAY.

At the end of the war Frank was deployed to Palestine along with his youngest brother, Dennis, they had survived the bombs, bullets, shelling, land mines, and then Dennis had to attend a Courts Marshall, he had suffered 'shell shock' (P T S D) and was charged with not coming to his senses while in charge of his rifle and crashing an Army vehicle. He was found not guilty but in time discharged on health grounds. Dennis died six years later in 1951 at the age of twenty five from Leukaemia.

I still have the letter Frank wrote to his sister (my mother) in 1946 from Palestine. He just wanted to get home from "This land of flies" Very seldom did Frank speak about D Day and what he experienced. The one time he did talk about it to me, he got emotional and cried. Most of his fellow soldiers and friends were either badly wounded or killed that day. He said the first scene in the film, 'Saving Private Ryan' depicted the carnage very well.

After the war Frank went back to his old job working as a butcher. He was married in 1947 to Dorothy Rigby. They had no children but Frank did have many nephews and nieces. Frank possessed a great sense of humour, he was pretty much self educated. He loved reading about Hinduism and Buddhism, he also liked philosophy and science. Frank was a good listener and he knew how to talk, on those subjects he had learned about.

He had practiced yoga most of his life, he followed football and was an ardent Liverpool fan, he was also a keen lawn tennis player. He played the guitar and loved jazz, but most of all he was an extremely likeable man. In my childhood days and as a young married parent, Frank was one man who's thinking and character, I was most influenced by. Frank died in 2006 and his ashes, my cousin. Peter, and I scattered along with his wife Dorothy's, who died 4 years earlier.

These seven young men of the time (yet to be my uncles) and their fellow combatants, had the experience of war, fear, comradeship and discipline. Memories that never left them, but they came through it better people. Not that, young people in particular, need war, violence and hardship to shape them, but in my view given the amount of realistic film and television violence we are all exposed to today, the bad language, the knife crime among school children and the drug scene, they do need as part of home discipline and school curricula, to be properly educated in social graces Ps and Qs and not take human life and what it has to offer for granted. They also need to be treated fairly and loved.

I learned from my uncle Frank that we live in two worlds at once, one of earth and rock, flesh and blood, the other, one's own world of values, ideas, beliefs, fears and superstitions. A world of thoughts and feelings, a world of love and hate, happiness and despair joy and sorrow. A world far removed from concrete and clay, where on the bigger world stage people like Ghandi and Mother Teresa quote from the wisdom of the past -

Ghandi:

'Our greatest ability as human beings, is not to change the world, but to change ourselves'

Mother Teresa:

'Not all of us can do great things, but we can do small things with great love'. and 'Peace begins with a smile'

The State (or moreover those who run it) in their attempt to cater for trade, business, the economy and the pastoral care (that once many decades ago, vocational bodies such as church and temple provided) fail to realise one major truth – Human flesh and blood can neither be bought or sold but must be looked after, in particular, the young and the old, and cared for by the family, the community and the bigger society of flesh and blood, in other words, us all, 'WE' go into making what we call 'The State'. From 'Us' are recruited the judiciary, the politicians, the journalists, the media, the police, the military, the business men, the trades people, the privileged, the under privileged, etc.etc.

It is a very poor reflection on society as a whole, that 'we' should be fed gossip, fake news and insincerity or by the unscrupulous self serving beliefs of a large number of present day media moguls, self interested politicians, businessmen and selfish oligarchs, who's belief in life appears to be that greed and competition generate wealth, that wealth is good, so therefore so is greed.. Politics rarely creates change, but people do and good people do, for the common good.

The Sikhs have a saying about politics:'Capitalism is the ideology whereby man exploits man, with Communism it's the other way around.'

Only when those in high office of responsibility begin to promote and broadcast policies, that not only cater for trade, finance and productivity, etc. but also address morals, customs and traditional family values and stuff like honesty, work ethic, dignity and self respect - the greatest good to the greatest number. Loud voices make the bigger headline, so there is arguing and shouting differences of opinion, which only serves to polarise the truth and create disunity.

I believe The Church, Temple and Synagogue, etc. are brick and mortar, built on hallowed ground, (for all of Earth is hallowed). They represent a retreat or haven whereby one can reflect, meditate or pray. They can generate atmosphere and induce feelings of peace and good will. They are silent – as is the wilderness. But holiness comes from within and is the one human experience that brings into existence these places of worship. This one sense of being, is what real Holy men and women, in centuries past and still today, have lived their lives for. It's what they, (with their self knowledge and wisdom) have led most of the world toward civilisation, faith and truth. Alas, in today's debate they too are silent or are being kept silent.

It could be said that religion is like the Highway Code, we adhere to when we drive. Though in some countries we drive on opposite sides of the road, we still follow rules of common sense, judgement and good will, for the benefit of road safety and the common good.

Some drivers may speed, some may drive recklessly for kicks, or jump a red light, some may seek the thrill of speeding but nevertheless one day they will grow up, mature and hopefully see the error of their ways before they kill or damage themselves or someone else. Endangering one's life and the lives of others, in the process of joyriding is like laughing at the altar. The people who wrote the Highway Code never had a code to go by, Just like those who wrote The Bible.

Who would deny youth their fun and games and on the other hand who or what can command ignorance, insecurity, despair?

With religion, one may say that it is a force for good as its main purpose is to nurture virtue and belief in God. Others might disagree and say it is the cause of conflict as it is so diverse and based on stories. Perhaps if we look at the etymology of the word 'Religion', it means 'to bind together' The word Eden, that the Judaeo / Christian Bible uses, means 'enclosure' look at it this way and it gives one a different perspective. Some other Biblical words for instance, the male name Adam; 'To tame' and the female Eve; 'The dawn of'

Though religious beliefs may be varied and tell different stories they all have one thing in common, they belong to the ancient past and to the storytellers. They are like different clothes and fashions, which change across the many varied cultures and eras that have existed since time began and still exist today. But all religious beliefs serve a purpose, like clothes, that keep us warm and modest they also protect us from temptation and indecency. Religion like politics, introspection and belief are all part and parcel of being human.

These subjects were never invented or thought up, but discovered within ourselves.

It is a human tragedy that the 'movers' of today's society since World War Two, have taken us down the path we have taken and chosen, through all the propaganda the weak values that have led to more and more street violence, selfishness and greed among us today and in particular among the young.

Humanity needs to be fed the food of virtue. In my view, belief is not like faith, as faith is not like knowledge, but we must have faith in others and in ourselves or else we could never experience the results of our ideas and beliefs that acquire knowledge (about ourselves). Replacing ignorance with knowledge is a process which sometimes requires believing in the impossible and having the courage, determination and faith, to gain insight into how to make the impossible, possible.

At the beginning of the twentieth century people said that man would never walk on the moon, a few decades later they were proven wrong.

What if it were the same with water?

Water to wine: To see the spectacular in the mundane
Walk on water: To rise above the ordinary

CONTENTS

CHAPTER 1
PRESENT DAY

The Mind of The Street

As children, playing
In the street outside
With friends and bikes
And playground rides,

Watched over by neighbours,
Mums or dads,
Boys chase the girls
Or laugh with the lads.

It's fun feeling free
And somewhat secure,
On moving away
From one's own front door,

Confidence building,
In the strong belief of
Still being watched over,
By something above.

Then somewhat older
And sometimes alone,
Among one's peers
And those unknown.

A new generation
Processed to meet,
Exciting ideas
Now out on the street.

Once, was the interest
In playing street games,
Now it's a matter
Of getting a name.

Or becoming a member
Of some kind of gang,
Using street language
And bad mouthed street slang.

Detached from their neighbours,
Their dads and their mums,
Taking up weapons
Like belts, knives, and guns.

It's the back alley culture,
Young kids on the street,
Like actors in a film shoot
All strive to compete.

They watch villain hero's
On film and T. V.
The excitement and drama,
Say, "That's what I'll be."

The need to be someone,
The need to look hard,
To show they've no fear,
To mark someone's card.

A hard case, a villain,
To garner respect,
It's what happens later
They never expect.

Young minds of the street
Portrayed as such,
The bad news reports
Becoming too much.

The dealing in drugs,
In violence and crime,
A far cry from younger
More innocent times.

Yet most of the kids
On todays city streets,
Are decent and kindly
And a pleasure to meet.

Beware of this savagery
And be on your guard,
Do not get caught up
In the ways of the yard.

Beware young people
When out on the street,
Beware of the mindless
Young villains you meet.

Beware, social media
Of a gossipy kind,
Can corrupt a young
And vulnerable mind.

Excitable language,
Vulgarity, sleaze,
Can be found in the alleyways
Out on the street.

On cell phones and tablets
Where rules don't apply,
Internet trolls send their crap
Through the sky.

Oh parents, oh parents,
Please be aware,
Of the dangers awaiting,
Your children out there.

The temptation, excitement,
The drama they face,
When having their fun and 'a laugh'
With their mates.

To prepare them beforehand,
Common sense, well advised,
Is essential to keep them
Safe and streetwise.

For todays city streets
Combined with 'The Net'
Is a challenge to all,
What is nurtured, they get.

Can't we be more protective ?
Try to stop all the rot,
Protect and encourage,
They are born violent not.

One asks what's the cause,
Have we all lost our way?
From those brighter times
When together, happy at play...

Can we no longer foster
A more humane peace?
To get rid of this violence
In the mind of the street.

Young Slaves to The Market

There are musicians and vocalists
And songwriters too,
Who'll sing and recite
For me and for you.

There are radio D.J.s
Promoters and those
Who ramp up production
Of music and prose.

There are beauticians, perfumeries,
Dressmakers and all,
With their needles and threads
Make us fit for the ball.

There are brewers, winemakers,
Wine tasters as well,
Charlatans, shamans,
Who add to the spell.

When we've danced and we've sung
And drank all night long,
When our pockets are empty
And we know not where it's gone.

We go back to the workplace
And brag to our friends,
Of the good time we've had,
Of how much we have spent,

The fruits of our labour,
The sweat and the tears,
Used social fodder
Throughout short, youthful years.

And as we grow old
Drunken violence still stands,
At the bottom of the hills,
Across our green land.

It's all bits of paper,
It never does stop,
Gets recycled, then returns
To all those at the top.

And we see no further
like fools that we are,
Those with no housing
Who carry the scar.

With zero hours contracts
And no future to aim for,
Young workforce of Britain
The new working, bred poor.

Social media and food banks
Are all that are left,
To stop them from protest
And from feeling bereft.

So they turn to their mobiles,
When nothing to do,
Absorbed in the net,
Filling their minds with other kids blues.

We're wined and we're dined,
We're all left behind,
Like young slaves to the market,
Conditioned, you'll find,

In our old age,
As we lay in our beds,
Riddled with illness
From the lives that we've led.

There are directors of funerals,
Florists and priests,
All play their part
In the ball and the feast.

What a waste of a nation,
What a waste of young lives,
Will we ever see sense,
Will we ever survive.

Why don't they give back
(Other than shares)
And build us a culture
Invested in care.

We need entertaining
Not treated like serfs,
Education with prospects
Is what we are worth.

But we're all being blinded
And lied to by those,
Who we trust in to lead us,
We are bought, spellbound and sold.

Yes go and enjoy life
But please be aware,
Of corrupt exploitation
That awaits us out there.

The Giants

Why is it
That we can see,
So much unfair inequality.
Throughout this land
From north to south,
Young people living
Hand to mouth.
From east to west
Shoppers greet,
Those sleeping rough
Out on the streets.
Taking hand outs
From you and me,
Seeking food banks
And charity.
Stepping back
I take a look,
Inside a Charlie
Dickens book,
And still today
Not out of place,
This land of ours
His stories grace.
While the tycoon giants
Have moved along,
They've left behind
This wanton throng.
It means we all are left behind,
While profits made are redefined.

Recycled not so all enjoy,
The dignity of their employ.
With services that all can share,
Housing, health, schools, welfare.
Instead the giants
Like Scrooge the miser,
Accrue profit and assets,
And we alas, are none the wiser.
The giant's share, not in the pot,
They keep their rewards
While young people rot.
Political parties know and see,
Yet fail to offer an equal, fair, economy.
The billionaire giants
No longer favour,
Culture investment, from their labour.
Far better for, the nation whole,
when we all give back
To reach that goal,
Prosperity !

War Games

War and violence, anger, hate,
PlayStation, Xbox,
Play it with your mate.
Imaginary violence sold for kids,
Excitement fosters anger hid.
Parents buy them they're 'harmless' they say,
Games of war, a sober way?
Pretending to harm, pretending to kill
Games of war is violence still.
Better to foster with our children's time,
Games of fun of a practical kind.
Not bombs and guns, killing and stuff,
On T.V. and movies if that's not enough,
The multi-nationals for profit, invent,
These games of violence for sale or for rent.
And we like fools, fall into the trap
And line their pockets, by buying their crap.

The Boat

Don't think money is protected
When we keep it in the bank,
And don't believe a person's wealth,
Commands a higher, safer rank.

And when we cast our voting rights
Is self interest on our mind ?
Think of what our culture needs
And all those left behind.

I don't mean that minority
Who for work have never cared,
I mean the vast majority
Whose voice is never heard.

They may say that higher taxes
Leaves less money there to chew,
Yet what of vital services
That's used by all the crew?

And what of equal justice
Education, transport, health?
Are not our savings best invested
In that of, the nations wealth?

Or should it be recycled
So it ends up in the hands,
Of that one per cent of people
Who wield the power of the land ?

The neoliberal advocates
Who sell us all the junk,
Are we not more worthy ?
Has the boat already sunk ?

Adverts

I wish there were more adverts,
I just can't get enough,
But they keep on interrupting
With that entertainment stuff.

I want to see more adverts
On my T.V. set,
But only T.V. programmes
Is all that I can get.

I'm wishing for more adverts
Though they're costly to produce,
I want to see them selling
Lemonade and orange juice.

And when I google something
It really makes me smile,
When their advertising pop-ups
Appear there all the while.

I only want more adverts,
Any kind would do,
Like nappies or viagra,
Coffee, tea or hair shampoo.

I find them entertaining,
I love them as they are,
But not the interruptions
Just to watch some show or star.

All those stories, documentaries,
Breaking news or such and such,
Soap operas, talent contests,
Chat show programs, far too much.

I'd rather watch the adverts,
They're so colourful and bright,
I like the ones on daytime
But mostly those at night.

In the night they show cars for sale,
Soap powder, burgers, beer,
Bet 365 and Paddy Power,
All the stuff we love to hear.

In the daytime there's commercials
For the older generation,
Electric folding scooters,
Chair lifts, pure cremation.

And when it comes to break time
And breaking news is on T.V.
I'll be in the kitchen
Eating biscuits, making tea.

Science and Space Exploration

Can they see them all these years
Science says have passed us by?
Yet they count them in their millions
For what purpose ? tell me why.
They can calculate the life span
Of the stars and show their worth,
Then predict at what will follow,
In the future, here on Earth.

Observing stars and the past,
Does this tell us, how long we'll last ?
The beginning of life (and me and you)
Studying this, cosmologists do.
What of our heavens' or our hell
Will this knowledge serve us well?
Will it cure us of our fears?
Will it rid us of our tears?
What of the cost of these endeavours?
In the billions I assume,
A nation might starve or struggle,
While sending probes beyond the moon.
They name this subject astro science,
It's the truth or so they say
Experimental observation,
So all else is thrown away .
No more creation, that's a story,
Not real at all, so we're told,
Once a thought to control us
In the past in days of old.

Evolution is the theory
Is the answer, so they say,
There's no need, for creation,
God has been and had his day.
No place for self or even wisdom,
Contemplation of the soul,
No need then for self reflection
We have knowledge, that's the goal.
Peace on Earth, it can't happen
So life's pleasures we must chase,
Survival of the fittest, fastest,
Is the practise we must face.
Invention of destructive weapons
Whose only purpose is to kill,
That give the rulers of their countries
Powers to, exact their will.
It's G.D.P. now and economics,
It's the order so adored,
Comforts that are so provided
Come from labour also gold.
The moral compass of those who rule us
Has somehow floundered, they've lost their way,
No more look for inner peace,
Bend the knee no more, or pray.
Fruit from the tree of human knowledge
Provides them with their bag of tools,
No more embrace such humble kindness,
No more embrace historic rules.
So be it, inflated egos
Lead us to mankind's extinction,
Weapons of such mass destruction,

This believe, is not a fiction.
Plus the carbon that we're burning,
Fossil fuels, CO_2
Climate change, Earth overheating,
Will life on Earth, make it through?
Can't they see we need a passage,
We need a door to nature's call,
To look inside ourselves, discover
Humanity, awaits us all.

People Rule

Are we, the people, used as fodder
Just to feed the marketplace ?
Spending wages from our labour,
While our rulers feed their face.

Would the price of oil just plummet,
Would the oilmen scream and groan,
If only for a week or two
'The people' stayed at home ?
Would the politicians listen,
Would they implement our needs?
Or would they carry on as usual
Turning blind eyes to the greed?
If we all stopped, social drinking,
Saying, "We're not finished yet"
Holding business to our ransom,
Then we stopped the urge to bet,
Would their empires come a crashing down?
Bringing justice to the fore,
Would we, the people, wear the crown
And multinationals rule no more?
Alas, our appetites and social life
Get exploited by all those,
Who don't Invest in public welfare,
As our weakness gets exposed.

But We Don't

We think we do but we don't,
We think we are but we're not,
We think we will but we won't,
We think we own what we got.

Democracy ?

We the public don't really rule,
We complain sometimes and moan,
We listen to our leaders
And they like us just groan.

For we are just the public
Whose vote they wish to garner,
So our politicians lobby us.
And we pick the greater charmer.

Then the party we elect
To deliver on their promise,
But of course their first objective
Is to satisfy the commerce.

And then we have the media,
Who just really want a scoop,
They lambast our politicians
And show how low they all can stoop.

It's easy to be cynical,
It's easy to complain,
Sometimes it's like a pantomime
And we're part of the game.

I'm sure lives could get better,
If only for a time,
If only each and all of us
Learned how to tow the line.

A 19th Century Factory Worker ?

Although I work to live more so than I live to work,
I care for the work I do and the company for
whom I work, all I ask in return is this:

That my company cares for me as a member of the workforce,
Rather, than careless to obsession with the force of work.

That my manager takes pride in his staff,
Rather, than staffs himself with pride.

That my manager takes the time to
listen to the men beneath him,
Rather, than it be beneath him to listen
or give to them his time.

That my foreman treats me with concern,
Rather, than concerns himself with contempt.

That my colleagues take interest in the work they do,
Rather, than disinterest in the job they are asked to do.

That if my colleague be loyal, trustworthy and responsible,
He be shown by his superiors the
recognition and respect he deserves.

And that God grant me the dignity
that comes with employment,
So I may endeavour to work for my employer until my death,
Rather, than be worked to death by my employer.

Benidorm

Is this modern hedonism?
High rise hotels to the sky,
Sunshine, beer, alfresco,
Sit and watch the world go by.

Hot dogs, booze and burgers,
Stand ups, karaoke, cabaret,
Drink all night to tribute acts
Until the break of day.

Enclosed by sea and mountains
Huge obelisks enfold,
Brits on tour, on holidays,
Stag Do's, families young and old.

The disabled in their mobile chairs,
The bare-chested with tattoos,
All sorts of shapes and sizes
Escaping from their blues.

Spanish natives make their living
From the tourist trade that's true,
To the business men of pubs and clubs
They are much a welcome crew.

And yet a mere distraction
From the beauty that surrounds,
The beach, the sea, the mountains,
And the picturesque Old Town.

Then high upon a hilltop,
A shining cross a saw,
Lighting up the dark night sky
Looking o'er the crowds, the sea, the shore.

Assassins

It happened many years ago
In Dallas, Texas, remember ?
Maybe you do, maybe not,
Of that fateful day in November.

The killing by a lone sniper,
The world was changed.
Was he crazy, mad,
Sick, deranged ?

No not Oswald,
He was just a man,
A shadow with a gun,
An assassin with a plan.

Killers of men
Like J.F.K. and Bobby too,
Martin Luther King, John Lennon,
To mention a few.

All killed with a gun,
Young men in their prime,
In full view their lives taken
Before their time.

And they know what they're doing
And the risks that they take,
These killers of men
For politics sake.

Those who they kill
In their serving, fall,
These crazy killers, have they
No conscience at all?

So why do they do it
What is it for?
And it's been done since
And been done before.

So how do they think,
What good does it do?
The dead just replaced
By the next in the queue.

So what's on their mind?
What do they believe?
Have they no feelings
Do they not themselves, ever grieve?

Have these killers no conscience ?
No sense of love,
Have they no families,
No God up above?

What does it take?
What does it need?
To stop all this violence,
Killing and greed.

To stop all these wars
And bring to an end
Fear and turmoil,
This inhuman trend.

For they never will walk
With a smile on their face,
With a sense of love
And a feeling of grace.

They never will know
What it's like to be free,
To have peace of mind
When one lets the world be.

CHAPTER 2.
REFLECTION

What Nature Has Wrought

Irrespective of belief, knowledge or thought,
We are all subject to what nature has wrought.
We all have our being by her code and law,
The process can't differ, though differ the form.
We are born, live and die in a short space of time,
We are what we are, needs must we comply. (with nature)
Only then can we see what life's all about,
See only the truth and eradicate doubt.
It's not what we think, what we know or believe,
But the fact that we can, that helps us perceive.

Faith

When gone are the days of childhood,
Of games and nursery rhymes,
Of chocolate and ice cream
And the bliss of childhood times,
When the times of adolescence
Have been and had their day,
And the older age of adulthood
Is here with us to stay,
Times of toil and hardship
And accountability,
Of parenthood, commitment
And the charge of what will be.
Times of sheer decision,
Of what is right and wrong,
Like the cold dark nights of winter
What one needs to get along,
Is a warm place by the fire,
With a nice hot cup of tea,
That's what one's faith will bring us,
Faith in what will be.
Make way then for our children
To live and have their day,
That they may come to cherish faith,
In God or Nature's way.

Seven Brothers

Seven brothers went to war
In Nineteen thirty nine,
What they said of what` they saw
Was not a nursery rhyme.

George and Harry, Charlie too,
Arthur, Leslie, Frank,
Dennis was the youngest,
Their mother's heart just sank.

In World War One, their father,
At the Battle of The Somme,
Suffered shrapnel to his leg,
Which he lost in years to come.

These men who fought a war abroad,
Three sisters left behind,
Husbands, wives and children
By fate they all survived.

The war when over, left its mark,
The cost, the story read,
In twenty years most were gone,
Six brothers, one sister, - dead.

Family men with wives and kids,
Gone while in their prime,
Taken by the illness,
Well before their time.

Was their illness caused by trauma ?
Their death was premature,
Was it from them suffering,
The affects of world at war?

And of the three that did survive,
Two sisters and a brother,
Only these were left alive
To comfort one another.

This horrific price of conflict,
The lasting cost of war
On the families of the innocent,
Who need a life of peace, much more.

Newly Born

To see what is heard,
To hear what is seen.
To dream of a life
That is living the dream.
To immerse in a taste,
The taste of a touch,
Absorbed by the sent
That is never too much.
Child senses so used
In varying ways,
Entwined with each other
Turning night into day.
The whoosh of a scent,
The hearing of sound,
To hear, touch, to see,
Human life found.

Within The Eyes of a Child

Nature has a secret
World wonders can't compare,
With that which lies within the eyes,
Of a child, and what's in there.

Perhaps

Perhaps we're here by accident,
Perhaps we're here by chance,
Perhaps a freak of nature
Born to question, think and dance.
Perhaps God is a make-believe
We cling to while we rot,
An early man invention?
Perhaps, but maybe not.

Character

Does ugliness deter you?
Does beauty blow your mind?
Or do you find that shades of grey
Are easier to find?
Do opposites attract?
Do likenesses repel?
Do race and creed and colour
Separate or gel?
Or is it that plain character
Defines just who we are ?
Nature over nurture
Mankind a settled par?
Is man born a savage
Or is he born humane?
Is fine character the nurtured cure
Or the source from which we came?

Freedom

Free to ask, free to talk,
Free to go where you want to walk.
Free to search, to seek and find,
Free to think and change your mind.
Free to believe in a greater good,
Free to do what you know you should.
Free to shout for freedom's fight,
Free to say what you know is right.
Free to follow not the crowd,
Free to be more than what you're allowed.
Free to be patient, modest, discreet,
Free to not seek attention, while out on the street.
Freedom for each, woman and man,
Freedom is this and yes, you can.

InTune

In tune with The Moon,
The Sun and the stars,
In tune with the Earth,
This Earth of ours.

In tune with the birds
And the fish of the sea,
In tune with each other
As it's meant to be.

In tune with the wildlife,
The wind and the rain,
In tune with oneself,
Put no one to blame.

In tune with the seasons,
With night and with day.
In tune with the moment,
With truth, not hearsay.

The Sinner and The Saint

Between sainthood and the sinner
There runs a slender line,
And we are quick to judgment
Almost all the time.

Our feelings tend to drive us,
Our actions take their course,
We seldom stop to take a breath
And seek our actions source.

Are they from the sinner
Or are they from the saint?
Are we trigger happy
Or do we show restraint?

Early Man

Dinosaurs and monster reptiles,
Savage nature at its worst.
One big struggle for these creatures,
No kind of life for man on Earth.

Is brutal man a made up story ?
Perhaps delusion, or a ruse ?
At best a guess to fit a picture,
To scare or to maybe, confuse.

When Man arrived, he found a jungle, paradise,
Among all creatures great and small,
A tribal man, a great inventor,
His woman and child was his all.

There is a place, a Fertile Crescent,
Where more likely man was born,
Where tribal culture truly flourished
And nurtured peaceful, passive, form.

Early man he faced no dangers
Only from the wilds of beast,
He learned to hunt to feed his family,
Bringing home a tasty feast.

Ate he fruit and vine and honey,
Ate he meat and fish and fowl,
Knew he not of time and money
Hunt he for the hog and jowls.

He learned to swim and catch a fish dish,
Navigated by the stars,
Made his camp by the water,
By a river, (a make-do spa)

They listened to the birds a singing,
They planted seeds, they gathered fruit,
Made they huts, discovered music,
Sang and danced, to a home made flute.

Tools and rules he created,
Invented language and wall art,
Taking shelter from nature's fury,
Humane kind began the start.

Took they shelter in the winter
In caves away from wind and storm,
Discovered fire and its uses
For cooking food and keeping warm.

Nurtured modesty and hygiene,
Buried, burnt, their dirt and waste,
Covered up with animal fur,
Tied with vines around the waist.

They named the oceans, made the wheel,
Discovered numbers, invented time,
Befriended dogs and tamed the horse,
And to the camel tied a line.

Observed the moon, observed the seasons,
Counted sunsets, named the days,
Charted stars and planted crops,
To feed their young and find their way.

Built they ships to sail the ocean,
Used the wind as it blew by,
Recognised dark clouds forming,
As they kept a watchful eye.

And nurtured they their little children,
Protect and feed their very young,
For many years this process happens,
'Till independence from child has sprung.

Turned dark to day to search the way
With fire torches, home made lighting,
Buried their dead, wrote down what was said,
With symbols, the start of reading, writing.

Entertained themselves with stories,
With legends and with nursery rhyme,
Created nouns for their surrounds
And then of course, invented time.

But tribal nature needs protecting
From its self and hostile tribes,
Mistrust, suspicion, self preservation,
Expansion caused the angry vibes.

Invented they destructive weapons,
Invented they the gun and bomb,
From clubs and slings, spears and arrows,
The path to self destruction comes.

Not until the tribes got bigger,
Not until they increased in size,
Did start the fight between each other,
Did warring factors start to rise

Left behind is a peaceful nature
Once desire for power looms,
Once humanity is weakened,
Fostered greed and anger, groomed.

Forgot us all of human virtue?
Forgot us all of love and peace?
So much discarded by our menfolk,
When will greed for power cease?

Ducks and Geese

The ducks and geese are all at peace,
At peace with nature's ways,
But the human mind has yet to find
Contentment, in its days.

The Illusion of Maya

Illusion or Fantasy
Delusion or dream?
A man made world
Where nature has been.
Concrete, plastic,
Synthetics and steel,
No longer the soul
Of the Earth do we feel.
Machinery, iron,
Skyscrapers and glass,
Cover the beauty
Of meadows and grass.
Aircraft, cruise-liners,
Cars, boats and trains,
Separate the vision
Of mind from the brain.
The word in Hindu
The Illusion of 'Maya'
Meaning 'Not This'
This man made layer.

The Hidden Soul

A world of peace and happiness,
Of contentment, calm and love,
Lay not outside our inner self,
Below us or above.

But closer than we choose to think
Yet not where thoughts may hide,
But inside one's humanity
Is where the soul resides.

Oh To Be As Children

Oh to see the world
Through the eyes of a child,
To lay there in wonder
Weeks born, still wild.

Oh to be as children
Playing on the grass,
Not thinking of the future,
Not fretting on the past.

Oh to be as children
When near to Christmas time,
Adults see the water,
Children see the wine.

Oh to be as children
Though weak and frail and small,
They have a power within themselves
That overcomes us all.

And as they grow, they lose it not,
Though smothered it may be,
By urge for power, ignorance,
And insecurity.

Yet though it wanes it can return,
Slowly, stage by stage,
With virtue, peace, contentment,
That come to some, with age.

All Are Human Beings

All are Human Beings,
Few are being Human,
All are for the 'seeing'
But the 'seeing' is for few men.

A Damascus Moment

Imagine while out walking
Or watching your T.V.
It suddenly appeared to you
Life is not, what seems to be.
You've missed the main perception,
Missed Mother Nature's theme,
Have buried that connection
And have lived a living dream.
Now you feel that you are floating,
Feel your problems have all gone,
You feel you've been uplifted
And a light on you has shone.
No feelings of oppression,
No ill thoughts, of any kind,
No worries with those negatives
That pop into your mind.
The way ahead is clear to you,
With yourself you're more at ease,
No longer do you feel entrapped,
The stress of life has ceased.
It's your Damascus moment,
At last you come to see
Just what it is you're born for,
Now at last, you're truly free.
And imagine if each one of us
Saw that light or sign,
Had that same experience,
In an instant, at one time.

Slow

A country walk in silence,
Through wind or rain or snow,
Peace bestowed, remembered,
When life, is taken slow.

I am Me

I am the dreamer
I am not the dream.
I am he who sees,
I am not who is seen,
I am the Walker
I am not the walk,
I am the talker
I am not the talk.
I am of the many
I am of the few,
I could be any
I could even be you.
I am what I was
I am what I'll be,
I am who I am
And what I call 'me'

I See Not

I see not the plastic
The concrete and the steel,
I see not the polythene,
They have no real appeal.

I only see the mountains,
The flowers and the trees,
I see only grassland,
The forests and the sea.

I see not the rail lines,
The trains, boats and planes,
I see not the motor cars
That clog up all the lanes.

I only see the sunshine,
The shining moon at night,
The stars and all the galaxies
A much more worthy sight.

I see not the office blocks
Rising to the sky,
I only see the wildlife
And the birds go flying by.

I see not the palaces,
The pavements and the streets,
I see not technology
But the world beneath our feet.

I see not the vanity,
The envy and the greed,
I only see humanity
And the love that we all need.

Unity

There is no heaven up above,
No hell down below,
There is no river to sail across,
No afterlife to know.
But this, believe is the truth,
This, believe no lie,
Life, is everlasting,
Even when we die.
The body is a carrier,
The mind is but a sense,
The self is what we really are,
Our lives are recompense.
Trust in our humanity,
Believe, in what we are,
Politics has never solved, or
Put right our wrongs so far.
Forgive, forget, move on again,
The past is not the goal,
Only here, only now
Comes unity with soul.

To Change The Way We Are

If we could change the way we are
And open up the heart ,
And show the wrongs to each we do
When the anger in us starts.

To show us all the violence
The ego in us does,
The selfishness & senselessness
For gain or for a buzz.

Do we think that it's acceptable
To inflict this harm and pain?
On strangers, friends and neighbours,
To off load the hate that we maintain.

Seldom is considered
To hold back and think again,
To turn away and let it go,
To let the urge just wane.

For we are not born savages,
We are human at the core,
Might we think of something greater,
Something better, something pure.

A Place to Live

When all mankind has ceased to be,
Has vanished in the mist,
When all man-made machinery
No longer does exist,
When all our pathways disappear,
Our buildings turn to sand,
When all what man has taken
Has returned back to the land,
There will be left behind on Earth
An awe-inspiring scene,
Rivers, lakes and mountains,
Wildlife running free.
Vegetation, fruit and vine,
Shores of golden sand,
Oceans, forests, valleys green,
Untouched by human hand.
Unpolluted lakes and streams,
A fragrant atmosphere,
No other place in all of space
With which one could compare.
Here would be the garden
Mother nature has, to give,
An island in a cosmic sea,
A perfect place to live.

All Embracing

Can the owl see darkness ?
Can the insect see shade,
Can the pig see the moonlight
Or man this facade ?

Can the fish see the water
See the ocean or the sea?
Can the blind man see his wisdom?
In his mind can he see ?

Can the ape see the beauty
In the stars up above?
Can it look to the past,
Forgive or fall in love?

Can man see his maker?
Or that which surrounds,
Embracing the all,
All light and all sound.

Knowing no boundary,
Knowing no end
And is its own witness,
And is its own friend.

Do we know that it's here?
In its shadow we live,
But we hardly give thought
For the life that it gives.

Two Hearts One Love

Two hearts one love,
One sky up above.
Two arrows one bow,
One archer, one goal.
Two songs, one tune,
One bride, one groom.
Two souls, one chance,
To live, love and dance.
Two rings, one sign,
He's hers, she's thine,
One bride, one groom.
One sun, one moon,
One bond, one cue,
Two words, "I do"
One Earth, one life,
One man, one wife.
One kiss, one caress,
All this, God bless.

CHAPTER 3
WE PEOPLE

The Lie

The little girl told a lie
And then she told another,
She told it to her sister
Then her brother, father, mother.
She liked to dream and fantasise,
She knew not the reason why,
The truth she felt, was boring
But she liked a little lie.
If her family then discovered this
It would only make her cry,
So they left her to her make-believe,
After all, it's just a lie.
She meant no harm and never felt
The years go passing by,
She kept on telling stories
And no one heard her cry.
The lies got her noticed though,
Many times she really tried,
But excitement's spell she fell for
And she couldn't stop the lie.
As an adult she continued,
It hurt, it really grieved her.
Even when she told the truth
Alas, no one believed her,
So the moral of the story is,
Look people in the eye,
Live a life of truthfulness
And ignore the urge to lie.

Forgiveness

No need for anguish,
For hurt or for pain,
When harsh words are spoken
It's always the same.
We always look somewhere
For someone to blame,
Don't fall in the trap,
Don't play that game,
Forgive us our egos
And keep your good name.
It's hard to forgive,
Feeling hurt, feeling harm,
Yet those who forgive,
Who extend out their arm,
Bring to themselves
Peace of mind, grace and charm.

Needs

One's physical needs are many,
One's comfort needs are few,
One's happiness needs, if any
Lay, with friends and family true,

The Country Folk of Eire

Every year on holiday,
Across the sea not far away,
To Diamond Valley in Little Bray,
With the country folk of Eire.

I stayed as a boy there on the farm,
Peace and love and a tranquil calm,
With my parents and siblings (and a host full of charm),
From the country folk of Eire.

Each summer I'd help bring in the hay,
Along winding lanes on a warm clear day,
On top of the bogie, my mind would stray,
Watching the clouds go by.

In the kitchen garden among the fruit,
With a goodly old lady of warm repute,
Strawberries, blackberries or whatever would suit,
For the jam she often made.

I'd play with the dogs with ball or stick,
Feed the pigs and the chicks,
Feed the cows, pull away real quick
When they tried to suck my fingers.

We'd stroll along the old blind lane
Until a bridge, a brook and a cottage we came,
Known as 'The Glen' by local name,
I'd play with the boys who lived there.

I'd help with delivery of milk from a van,
In churns and urns with a kindly man,
He was wise and I, was a really big fan,
He had such a great sense of humour.

The Bramley folk would often come over
And picnic there amongst the clover,
Tell stories, jokes, on Mount Carraigoona
In the beautiful Wicklow mountains.

Little Sugarloaf or Big Bray Head,
Walk to the top or take the chair lift instead,
Laughing tears were often shed,
With the country folk of Eire.

The Dargle River and Broderick's well,
At Diamond Valley I was under its spell,
In love with this place I always fell,
And the country folk of Eire.

I went again on honeymoon,
Always welcome always room,
Then as a family with our children we groomed,
Like the country folk of Eire

Something

I am not my body
Though my body reflects me,
Like I am not the words I use
Or the things I say and see.

I am not the judge
Of all that's wrong or right,
And we are not the fighters
But we are part of the fight.

We are not are brains we use
Nor the thoughts that we may think,
Humanity is the boat we sail
By which we float or sink.

We are not the stories
That we hear from time to time,
We are not the pain we feel,
When 'they' step out of line.

We are not just objects
Or fantasies of mind,
We were not born savage,
We are of human kind.

There's something good in each of us,
If we could only be,
More conscious of its presence,
What a world this world would be.

The Spirit Self

Through the mother's womb the body comes,
From this mankind is born
And from the body, as it grows,
The spirit self is shorn.

Moving On

There's a world that we're awake to
And to one that we're asleep,
The one we often think of
And where our dreams we keep.
When our waking world is hurtful,
Where no longer we find love,
We dream of where we'd rather be
And that care we're thinking of.
We may choose to take some time out,
To get away from all the pain
And travel to a better place,
To feeling free and young again.
But that's just the world of dreaming,
That rarely does come true,
So back into this wakeful world
But no need to feel so blue.
For it's the only one we're born to,
So it's really up to us,
Ignore the pain, stand up again,
Move on, don't park the bus.

The Need To Sing

We need to sing, we need to hum,
To the beat of the rhythmic circadian drum,
where the birds sing and dance
In a natural trance,
Live life, play games,
Feed and drink, have fun.
We need to not look
To the past anymore,
Or to the future
But go through the door
Of present day times,
Released from our crimes
By forgiveness from each,
Under our own, humanity's law.
We need to move on,
Grow up and mature,
Go seek and find ourselves, once more.
The treasure that lies so locked away
In peace and love,
Would change us all forever more.

The Prize

How can the cause be lost,
When in one's heart
One holds The Prize?
And it can take a lifetime
Which is the price, the cost,
The time that it can take
To see this worldly vanity,
And in oneself, experience its demise.

Peace,
This peace which has always been,
That which pygmy ego strives to smother,
Thus, awakened from that dream
And now, placed in another.

I Wonder

I wonder if the time will come
When everyone on Earth,
Recognise just what we are
And the value of our worth.
I wonder when events occur
Through nature or through men,
Humanity is revered by all,
What will our lives be then.
I wonder when the minds of most
Will see the light of day,
Will put to bed their egos
And their superstitious ways.
I wonder when hostility,
Violence, hate and greed,
Will evaporate and fade away
And humanity succeed.
For I am not alone in this
As lots of people know,
The type of world that can be had
When grace and goodness grow.

I Am Human

I am greater than the snake,
Greater than the ape,
Greater than the oceans,
The mountains and landscape.
For none of these look back at me,
And question what it is they see.

We Are Human

We are human,
We make mistakes,
But what it takes
Is to show remorse,
To compromise, apologise,
Forgetting not,
Forgiveness, of course.

The Hangover

Tell me where am I ?
Last night is a blurr
I know I went out
But I know not where.
I must have got home
But I know not how,
I remember some drunkenness
And music so loud.

Did I have a good time ?
I hope that I did,
It cost me a fortune
At least eighty quid.
I fell and went over
A friends garden wall,
That's where I slept,
Not one heard my call.

I dragged myself up
And staggered along,
A cold, rainy night
And singing a song.
I met a tall policeman,
He said he could tell,
Drunk and disorderly
I got locked in a cell.

I said I know not
The hell where I live
And the name Mickey Mouse
Was the one that I give.
I think I got rescued
By my wife's friend and spouse,
Who bailed me out
Took me home to our house.

And to sleep it off
My wife put me to bed,
I woke up and I shouted
Take this pain from my head.
So never again
I feel so unwell,
My pockets are empty
With a hangover from hell.

No never again
We've all heard it before,
It's not very clever
A night's drunken, pub tour.
As I come to my senses
And walk down the stairs ,
Over stained clothes and vomit,
She's standing right there.

Now I'm slowly coming 'round
The music to face,
I wish I was elsewhere
Not here in disgrace.
Her face is like thunder
With eyes that could kill,
Was it so wrong to ask her,
If she loved me still.

CHAPTER 4
A SHORT STORY

THE WORD

Part One
Once there was a word
Yet its sound remained unheard,
Its partner was a light
Yet no eye had traced their flight.
'Something' moved them and they sang,
Emanating, in a bang.
Stars and comets everywhere.
Above, below, space and time,
Like something from a nursery rhyme.
Between the two they both gave birth,
An egg was born, fire, earth,
Planets forming, water, air,
And Earthly life commenced to stir.
Then as a star shone from above
(As if with Earth it were in love)
Rain clouds, water, came to form,
The beginning of that early storm.
Drowning rain commenced to pour,
Earth was shaken to the core.
Seas and ocean, waves climbed high,
Violent winds blew in the sky.
Hurricanes, tsunamis, lightening,
Volcanic lava, scenes so frightening.
Thunder, floods, windswept destruction,
From the earthquakes came construction.
Mountain ranges slowly formed,
Land turned green, blue sky adorned.
The storm had passed and in its place,

Tranquil beauty, peace and grace.
Streams and rivers in a single flow,
Into the valleys and lakes below.
Where fruit and vine commenced to grow.
And there was day and there was night
Yet still no eye for stars so bright.

Part Two
Vegetation grew
To feed those creatures who
Were forming in the sea,
While insects, flowers, trees,
Butterflies and bees,
Were laying the foundation
For a diverse inundation
Of creatures who came forth,
Opening the door
To an unspoilt, unseen view,
Of an unfenced, immense zoo.
Aeons passed in time and so
Life on Earth would ebb and flow.
And Then —-

Part Three
There came a man
Who spoke and said, "I am"
With no knowledge or awareness
Of that which came to bare us.
Yet he could speak and laugh and cry,
Love and hope and question why.
He questioned all that which he saw,

Just like now but even more.
He searched around, looked at the sky,
A tear flowed out, from of his eye.
And so he set himself a goal,
With his body, mind and soul,
To fly up high among the stars
And then look down on Earth because
It seemed that we, the human race
Were deemed unwelcome in this place.
A weaker species , our remit -
We didn't seem at all to fit,
With apes, gorillas, chimpanzees
And land mass animals such as these.
But he could think, believe and feel,
Create and sing and speak, reveal,
Make music, laugh and plan and play,
Create and work by night or day.
Make fire from the very start,
Symbols, writing, tools and art.
Intelligence of man supreme,
Live and love and trust and dream.

Part Four
With his woman by his side
Human kind would live and die.
In time his number multiplied,
He overcame, he occupied (Earth)
And he was white and black and brown,
And all spoke they with different sound.
In eras past when Earth was young
And Human life had not long sprung,

The sun would rise and then would set,
The dark brought fear and sense of threat.
To build, erect and to create,
Humanity was made to wait,
Superstition, acts of vice,
Pagan worship, sacrifice.
Anger, violence, slavery,
Hedonistic revelry.
Slow to spring from realisation,
Godly worship, civilisation.
Prophets brought them faith and hope,
And with their demons helped them cope.
Some spoke of doom and warring ways,
Apocalypse and end of days.
On this our Earth with stars above,
A glimmering sense of inner love.
The tree of knowledge, the fruit it bore,
Days of science, times of war.
Opposing beliefs, the urge to fight,
The savage mind, believing all, that they were right.
So came division, derision, suspicion.
It clouded their minds and blinded their vision.
Superstition and violent tongue,
Listened to, by the very young.

Part Five
As years and eras passed them by,
So advanced his task, his climb.
Science, technology, came to the fore,
He prised wide open nature's door.
Telescopes and microscopes,

The knowledge brought him highest hopes.
Trains and cars and aeroplanes,
Weapons, bombs and spacecraft flame.
He left one day his mother's womb,
Far from Earth now on the moon.
Erecting stations in the sky,
So to the planets he could fly.
He travelled far and scoured wide,
Around the cosmos with self inside.
Sending probes beyond the sun,
To seek out life, but he found none.
Only silence everywhere,
Now in this dawn, more self aware.
He looked with awe into the night,
Through the darkness and the light.
This cosmic universe so vast,
Infinity he now unmasked.
Before him there so stood the void,
The cosmic sea had now destroyed
His ego and this vane desire,
Humility, at last leapt higher.

Part Six
So came the hour to return,
Go back to Earth, begin again.
He moved in time, he moved in space,
He stared at life right in the face.
There ahead and high above,
An oasis, peace, a place to love.
A beautiful orb of shining hue,
A place to live and coloured blue.

A place to be, a place to die,
A place to ask and question why.
He knocked and opened was the door,
He vowed no more to go to war.
Off he cast on bended knee
His foolish past he'd come to see.
Anger, hatred and despair,
This endless search for life out there.
No more killing, no more shame,
Just humbleness, reborn and tame.
He arrived on Earth now filled with joy,
A Human Being, a man, a boy.

Part Seven
As he stepped down from his ship,
Weary from his eerie trip,
He felt the air against his skin,
The roaring silence flowed within.
He stood alone, all one was he,
A sense of peace and he could see,
Valleys green and sky of blue,
Flowers, birds and morning dew.
He looked around at nature's trees,
At nature's mountains, nature's seas.
At given rivers, given lakes,
At given life and all that makes
This place we live, this place we stand,
Beneath the sky, above the land.
He'd come to grips with that which is
And grasped at last what's really his,
He heard The Word, imagine this,

He saw The Light, this heavenly bliss,
Now all that's left for him to do
Was tell the rest of what he knew.
How long this took he could not tell,
Mankind, was under nature's spell.
But then again, he was not the first,
To self enlighten and taste it's thirst.
And so the cycle carries on,
'Till each alone, one by one,
To see, to know, to come aware,
Of when each one, the soul they share.
When self is reconciled with fact
And truth is realised at long last,
All together, yet each alone,
Living here on Earth, our home.

THE END

ACKNOWLEDGEMENTS

Though there are a number of people I should thank for their love, support and education growing up throughout my life, family, friends, etc. I have chosen four men who I was lucky enough to have had as role models and who influenced my way of thinking.

Every day we are surrounded by people who have an impact into what we become. When growing up, we are all role models to each other, good and bad.

Frank Cammack was the one man who got me interested in Far East culture. We had endless discussions on Buddhism, Hinduism, Christianity and world religions in general, Philosophy and self-awareness. I sat with him in the final hours of his life, in the hospice he was transferred to from hospital, suffering from cancer.

My cousin Paddy, who my family stayed on holiday with and his parents and sister, at Diamond Valley Farm, almost every year through my childhood and two or three times with my wife and children. A man full of wit, humour and compassion. In his spare time he helped run a boxing youth centre.

My good friend and colleague, Wally, who unconsciously imparted his streetwise awareness to me, in conversations in the car, on those cold, icy, winter mornings on our way to work, in the 70s, 80s, and 90s.

And finally Father Stephen, of Our Lady's Church, Runcorn, for being a role model of a man in a spiritual sense, to me he was more than a member of the clergy, despite being a priest, he too was streetwise, straight away likeable (and what seemed to me to be, at peace with the world).

SEVEN SERVING SONS

George.

Harry.

Charlie.

Arthur.

Leslie.

Frank.

Denis.

Mr. and Mrs. George Cammack, of 68a Aigburth Road, Liverpool 8, have seven sons doing their bit. Mr. George Cammack says they are only chips of the old block, as he served in the R.A.M.C. in the last war from 1914-1919. The sons are George, aged 36, R.A., wounded at Dunkirk; Harry, aged 32, in an anti-aircraft unit; Charlie, aged 29, who fought in the rearguard at Dunkirk with the Prince of Wales' Volunteers; Arthur, aged 28, in the 8th Loyals; Leslie, aged 24, Royal Engineers; Frank, aged 18, Home Guard; and Denis, aged 15, Civil Defence Cadets.

A cutting from the Liverpool Post and Echo in 1941